W9-BLI-549

Dominican Republic

by Rachel Anne Cantor

Consultant: Karla Ruiz
Teachers College, Columbia University
New York, New York

BEARPORT
PUBLISHING

New York, New York

PARK FOREST PUBLIC LIBRARY 60466

Credits

Cover, © glenda/Shutterstock and © Peter Elvidge/Shutterstock; TOC, © Maciej Czekajewski/Shutterstock; 4, © Maciej Czekajewski/Shutterstock; 5T, © Daniel-Alvarez/Shutterstock; 5B, © Holger Mette/iStock; 7, © photopixel/Shutterstock; 8–9, © Tom Bean/Corbis; 9R, © diegobib/iStock; 10–11, © tandemich/Shutterstock; 10L, © Andrew Bassett; 11R, © Eladio Fernandez/NHPA/Photoshot/Newscom; 12T, © Universal Images Group/DeAgostini/Alamy Stock Photo; 12B, © Everett Historical/Shutterstock; 13, © trappy76/Shutterstock; 14–15, © Frances M. Roberts/Newscom; 16, © Dikoz2009/Dreamstime; 17, © Massimo Dallaglio/Alamy Stock Photo; 18L, © sursad/Shutterstock; 18R, © Andris Tkacenko/Shutterstock; 19, © Robert Harding World Imagery/Alamy Stock Photo; 20–21, © photobeginner/depositphotos; 22T, © bonchan/Shutterstock; 22B, © rmnoa357/Shutterstock; 23, © Clara Gonzalez/Shutterstock; 24, © Steve Collender/Shutterstock; 25, © epa european pressphoto agency b.v./Alamy Stock Photo; 26, © PKM1/iStock; 27T, © PaulaConnelly/iStock; 27B, © Tarzhanova/Shutterstock; 28–29, © Danita Delimont/Alamy Stock Photo; 29B, © Timmary/Shutterstock; 30L, © dchulov/depositphotos; 30R, © Asaf Eliason/Shutterstock and © mumbojumbo/Shutterstock; 31 (T to B), © photobeginner/depositphotos, © Everett Historical/Shutterstock, © yanikap/Shutterstock, © Robert Harding World Imagery/Alamy Stock Photo, and © Maciej Czekajewski/Shutterstock.

Publisher: Kenn Goin
Editor: Jessica Rudolph
Creative Director: Spencer Brinker
Design: Debrah Kaiser
Photo Researcher: Olympia Shannon

Library of Congress Cataloging-in-Publication Data

Names: Cantor, Rachel Anne, author.
Title: Dominican Republic / by Rachel Anne Cantor.
Description: New York, New York : Bearport Publishing, 2016. | Series:
    Countries we come from | Includes bibliographical references and index. |
    Audience: Ages 4–8.
Identifiers: LCCN 2015037732| ISBN 9781943553334 (library binding) | ISBN
    1943553335 (library binding)
Subjects: LCSH: Dominican Republic—Juvenile literature.
Classification: LCC F1934.2 .C37 2016 | DDC 972.93—dc23
LC record available at http://lccn.loc.gov/2015037732

Copyright © 2016 Bearport Publishing Company, Inc. All rights reserved. No part of this publication may be reproduced in whole or in part, stored in any retrieval system, or transmitted in any form or by any means, electronic, mechanical, photocopying, recording, or otherwise, without written permission from the publisher.

For more information, write to Bearport Publishing Company, Inc., 45 West 21st Street, Suite 3B, New York, New York 10010. Printed in the United States of America.

10 9 8 7 6 5 4 3 2 1

JUN - 1 2016 DIRECT

Contents

This Is the Dominican Republic .. 4

This Is the Dominican Republic

Sunny

Friendly

BUSY

The Dominican Republic is a **tropical** country.

It's located on the island of Hispaniola.

The island is in the Caribbean Sea.

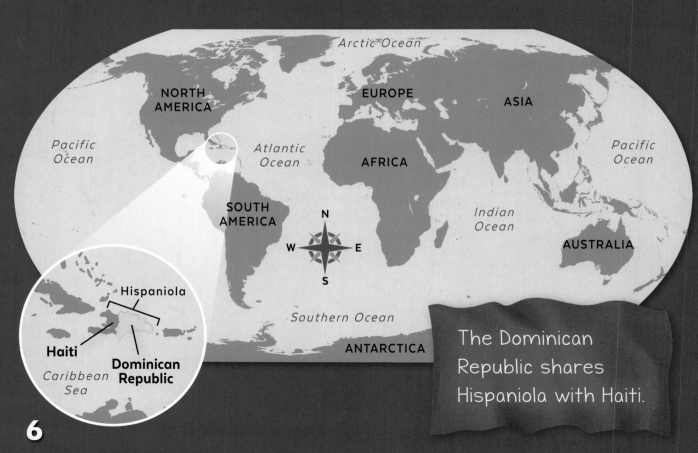

Arctic Ocean

NORTH AMERICA

EUROPE

ASIA

Pacific Ocean

Atlantic Ocean

AFRICA

Pacific Ocean

SOUTH AMERICA

N

W   E

S

Indian Ocean

AUSTRALIA

Southern Ocean

ANTARCTICA

Hispaniola

Haiti

Dominican Republic

Caribbean Sea

The Dominican Republic shares Hispaniola with Haiti.

Caribbean
Sea

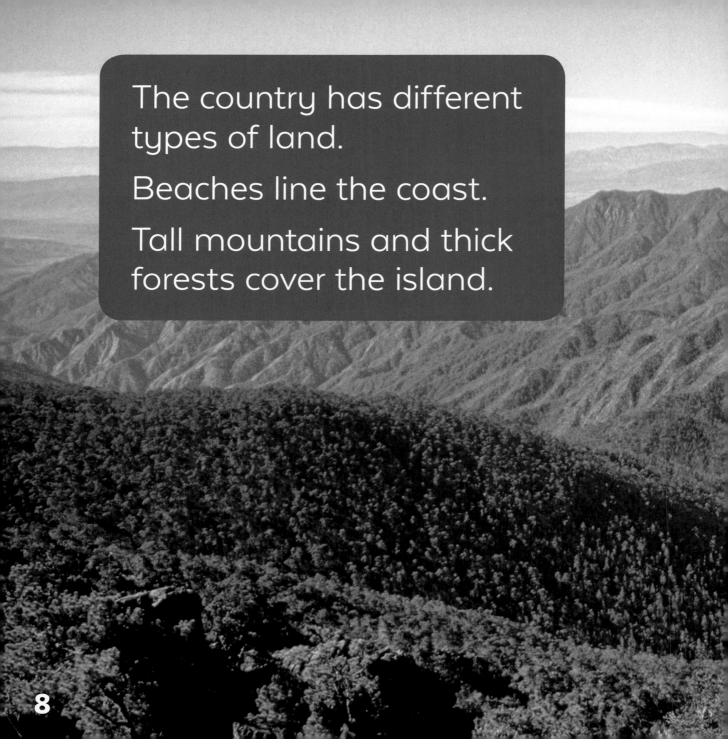

The country has different types of land.

Beaches line the coast.

Tall mountains and thick forests cover the island.

The Dominican Republic has many beautiful waterfalls.

The country's forests are filled with amazing animals.

Huge lizards hide under plants.

Colorful parrots live in trees.

parrot

The solenodon (suh–LEE–nuh–don) lives on the forest floor. This furry animal has a poisonous bite!

The Taíno (TYE-noh) were the first people to live on Hispaniola.

A cave drawing made by the Taíno

In 1492, Christopher Columbus arrived.

Christopher Columbus

He set up a Spanish **colony**.

The Spanish brought slaves from Africa to the island.

The Spanish built many churches. Some of them are still used today.

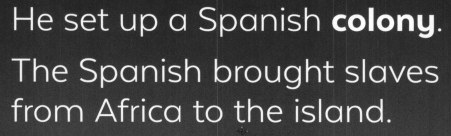

Spain lost control of the colony in 1821.

Then Haiti ruled the island.

In 1844, Dominicans won their freedom from Haiti.

Dominicans celebrate their freedom with parades.

Most Dominicans speak Spanish.

How do you say *please* in Spanish?

Por favor (PORE fah-VORE)

Many Dominicans also know some words in African and Taíno languages.

This is how you say *thank you*:

Gracias (GRAH-see-uhss)

17

Some Dominicans work on farms.
They grow plants such as cacao
(kuh-KOU).

Cacao is used to make chocolate.

cacao plant

chocolate

Other people work in **tourism**. They help visitors in stores and restaurants.

19

Santo Domingo is the country's **capital**.

It's also the country's biggest city.

About three million people live in Santo Domingo!

Dominicans eat many kinds of tasty foods.

Some meals are made with plantains.

This fruit is similar to bananas.

plantains

Fried plantains can be salted and eaten like chips.

Mangú is made of mashed plantains.

Dominicans celebrate many holidays.

Family and friends get together on Christmas.

They often decorate with lights.

Dominicans celebrate Christmas for three months!

people looking at Christmas decorations in a park

25

A rare material called amber is found in the Dominican Republic.

It's formed from tree **resin** over millions of years.

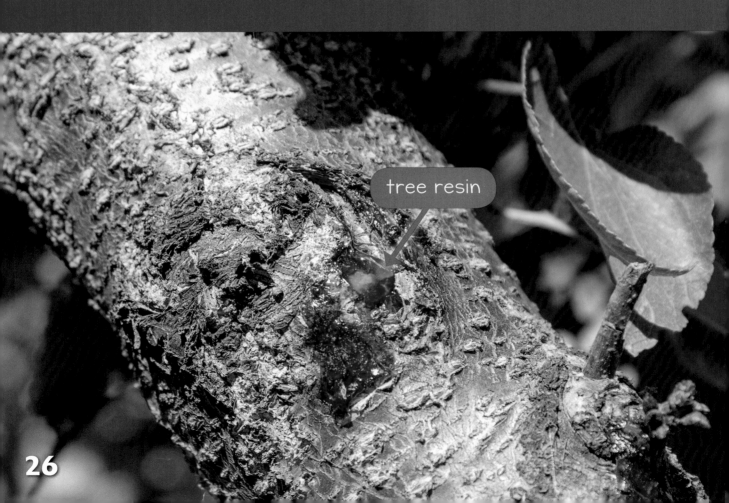

tree resin

ants

Sometimes, ancient insects are found trapped inside amber!

Amber can be made into jewelry.

What's the most popular sport in the nation?

Baseball!

Many people love to play and watch this game.

Soccer is also a popular sport.

Fast Facts

Capital city:
Santo Domingo

Population of the Dominican Republic: More than ten million

Main language: Spanish

Money: Dominican peso

Major religion: Catholic

Neighboring country:
Haiti

Cool Fact: Santo Domingo is the largest city in the Caribbean.

capital (KAP-uh-tuhl) a city where a country's government is based

colony (KOL-uh-nee) an area that has been settled by people from another country and is ruled by that country

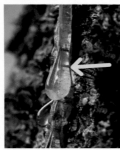

resin (REZ-in) a thick, sticky liquid released by some trees; over time, resin can harden into amber

tourism (TOOR-iz-uhm) the practice of traveling and visiting places for fun

tropical (TROP-ih-kuhl) having to do with the warm areas of Earth near the equator

Index

Read More

Rogers, Lura, and Barbara Radcliffe Rogers. *Dominican Republic (Enchantment of the World).* New York: Scholastic (2009).

Simmons, Walter. *The Dominican Republic (Blastoff! Readers: Exploring Countries).* Minneapolis, MN: Bellwether Media (2012).

Learn More Online

To learn more about the Dominican Republic, visit
www.bearportpublishing.com/CountriesWeComeFrom

About the Author

Rachel Anne Cantor is a writer who lives in New Jersey. She hopes to visit the Dominican Republic sometime soon.